How Did You Hear That?

MICHÈLE DUFRESNE

TABLE OF CONTENTS

What Is Sound?	2
How Sound Moves	8
Animals and Sound	10
Sound and Music	16
Glossary/Index	20

PIONEER VALLEY EDUCATIONAL PRESS, INC

WHAT IS SOUND?

Do you like to listen to music?

Do you like to hear birds singing?

Do you like to talk to your friends?

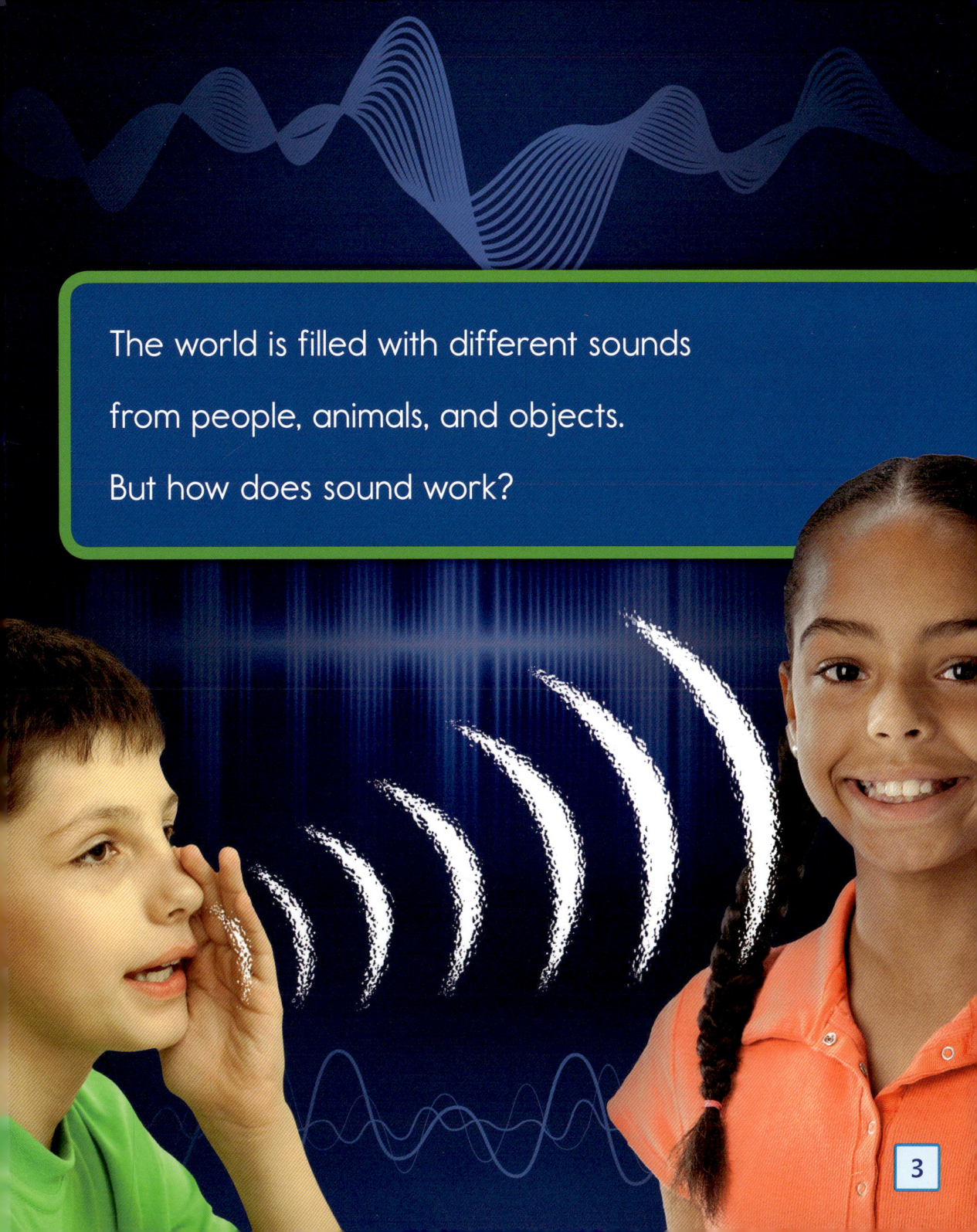

The world is filled with different sounds from people, animals, and objects. But how does sound work?

Gently place your hand on your throat and hum a little song. Do you feel a **vibration**? That feeling is caused by tiny **particles** moving back and forth. Sound is carried through the air when those particles push against other ones.

If you throw a rock into a pond, it will create waves shaped like rings. This is how sound works. The vibrations make sound waves. The waves move through the air and into our ears.

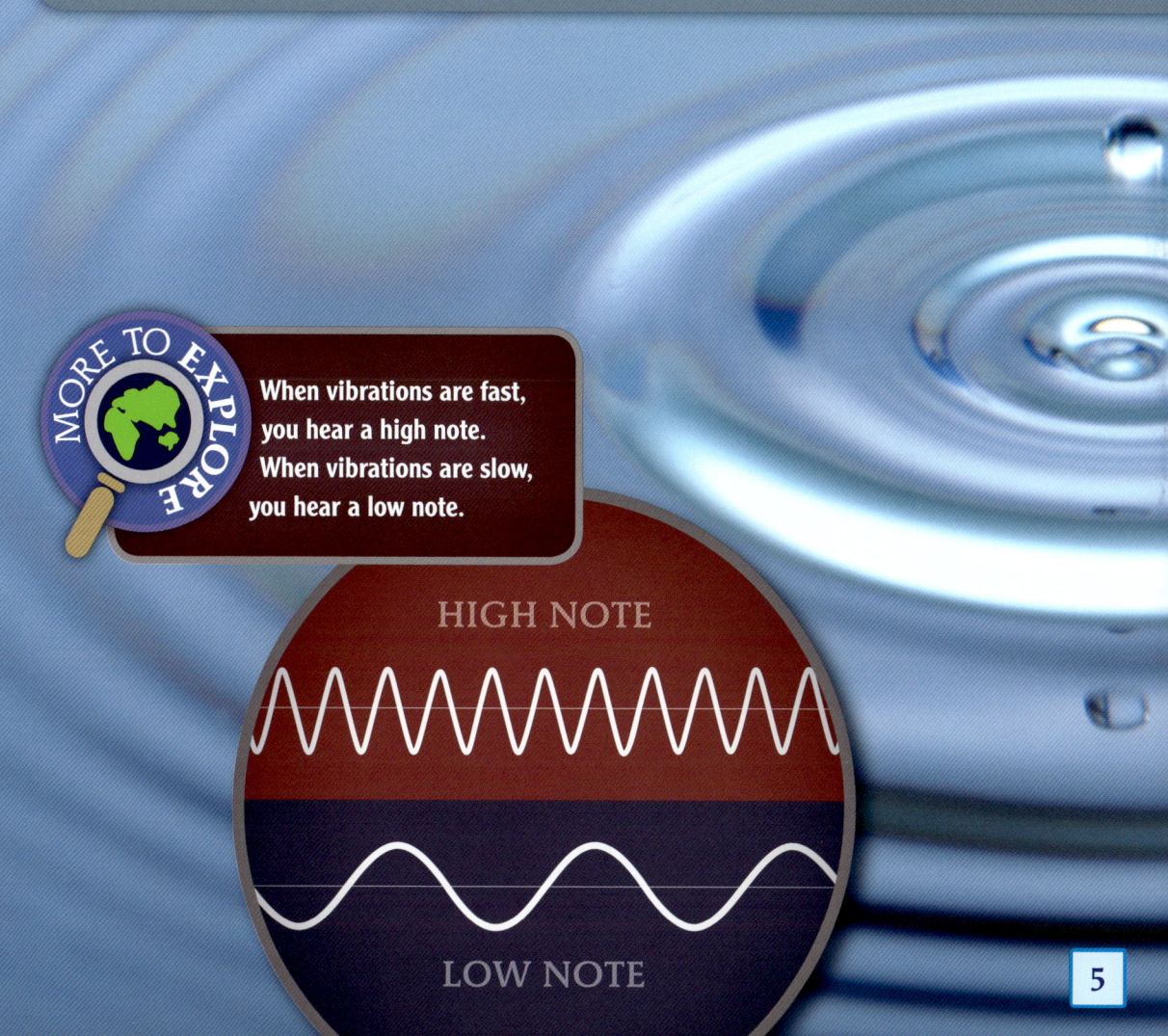

MORE TO EXPLORE
When vibrations are fast, you hear a high note. When vibrations are slow, you hear a low note.

HIGH NOTE

LOW NOTE

How do you hear a sound? Your ears catch sound waves and pass the vibrations down to tiny hairs inside your ear. This sends a message to your brain that describes the noise you heard.

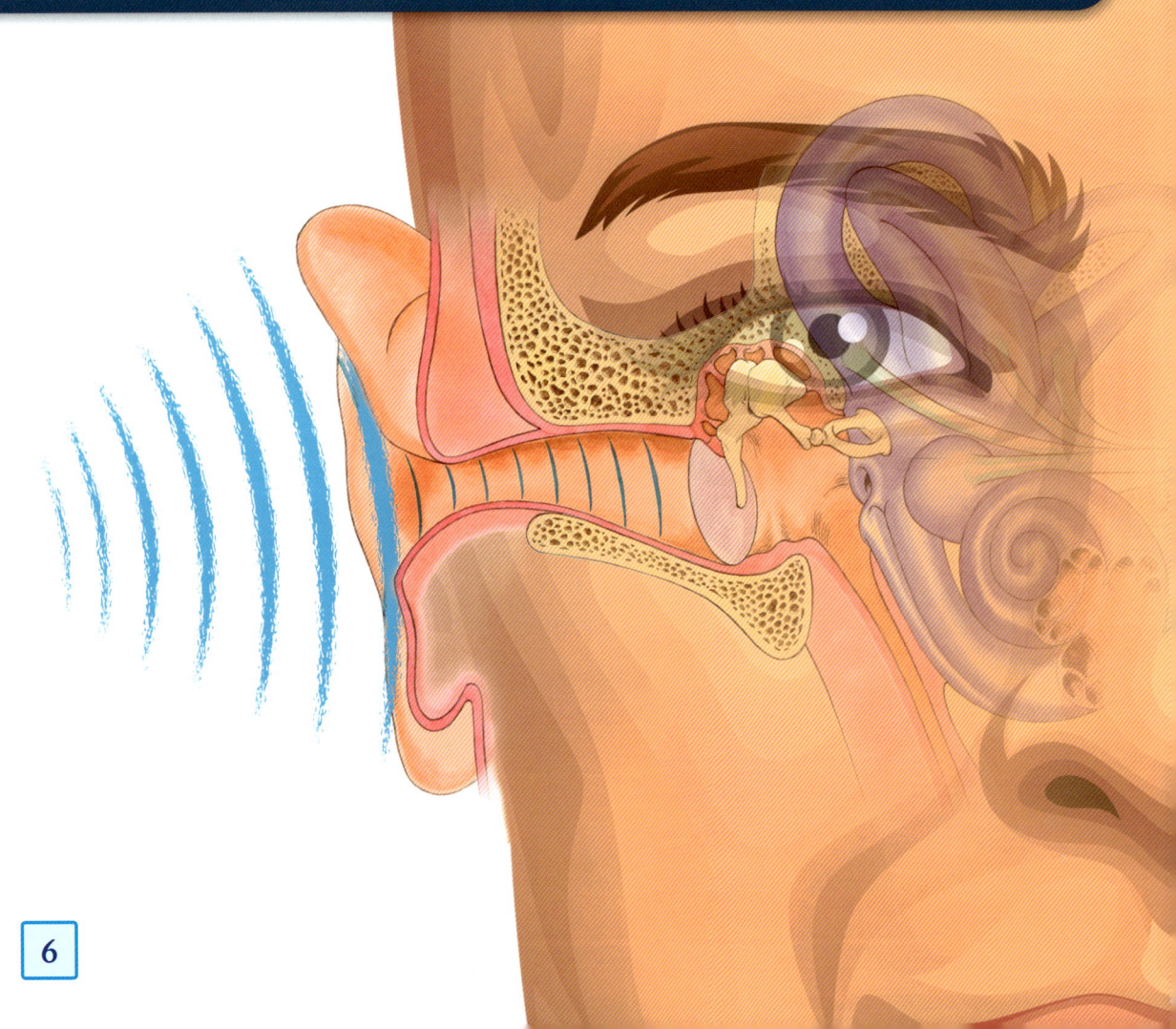

If a sound is soft, the hairs will only move a little. If a sound is loud, the hairs will rock back and forth very fast. Some sounds are so loud that they damage the hairs. Ears with damaged hairs will not pick up as many sounds.

HOW SOUNDS MOVE

Sound can travel through almost anything.

It can travel through a liquid, like water, or through something solid, like the walls in your house.

It can also travel through air.

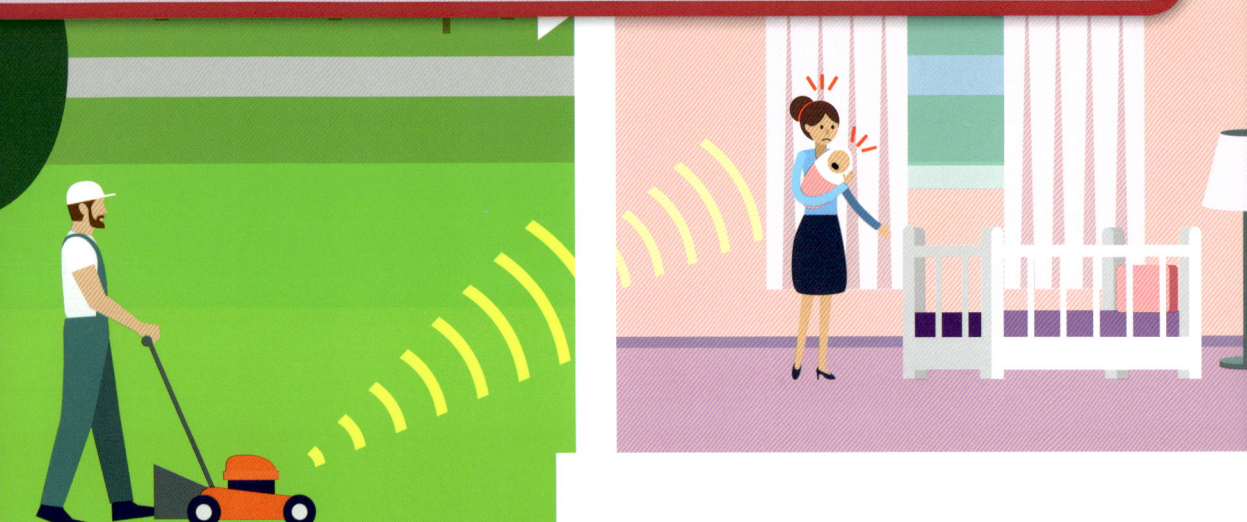

Sound can travel through water. In fact, it travels four to five times faster through water than it does through air.

Light travels much faster than sound.

This is why you see lightning before you hear thunder.

They happen at the same time,

but the sight of lightning travels to your eyes

before the sound of thunder can travel to your ears.

MORE TO EXPLORE

When a volcano in southern Asia erupted in 1883, the sound of the blast was so loud that people in Africa heard it. The sound traveled all the way across the Indian Ocean!

ANIMALS AND SOUND

Sound is very important to animals.

Many animals' ears are designed for a certain purpose.

They might pick up the sound of prey nearby

or a predator quietly following them.

Have you ever heard someone say,

"I'm as blind as a bat"?

Bats have poor eyesight, but they have excellent hearing. They use sound to find food. When they make a high-pitched sound, the vibrations crash into objects around them and bounce back as an echo. This is called **echolocation**.

The greater wax moth has the best known hearing of any animal. Scientists think these moths use their extraordinary sense of hearing to escape from bats. The greater wax moth can hear the bat and fly away.

Whales use sound in the same way that bats do. Whales make clicking sounds to locate objects underwater. The vibrations they hear can tell them if the object is near or far. Sometimes it can even tell them if the object is a friend or an enemy.

Whales can hear one another when they are very far apart.

A dolphin can hear seven times better than people.

SOUND AND MUSIC

When you blow into some instruments, like a flute or a trumpet, the vibrating air makes sound.

To play a stringed instrument, such as a guitar or violin, move the strings to make them vibrate. Shorter strings create higher sounds. Longer strings create lower sounds.

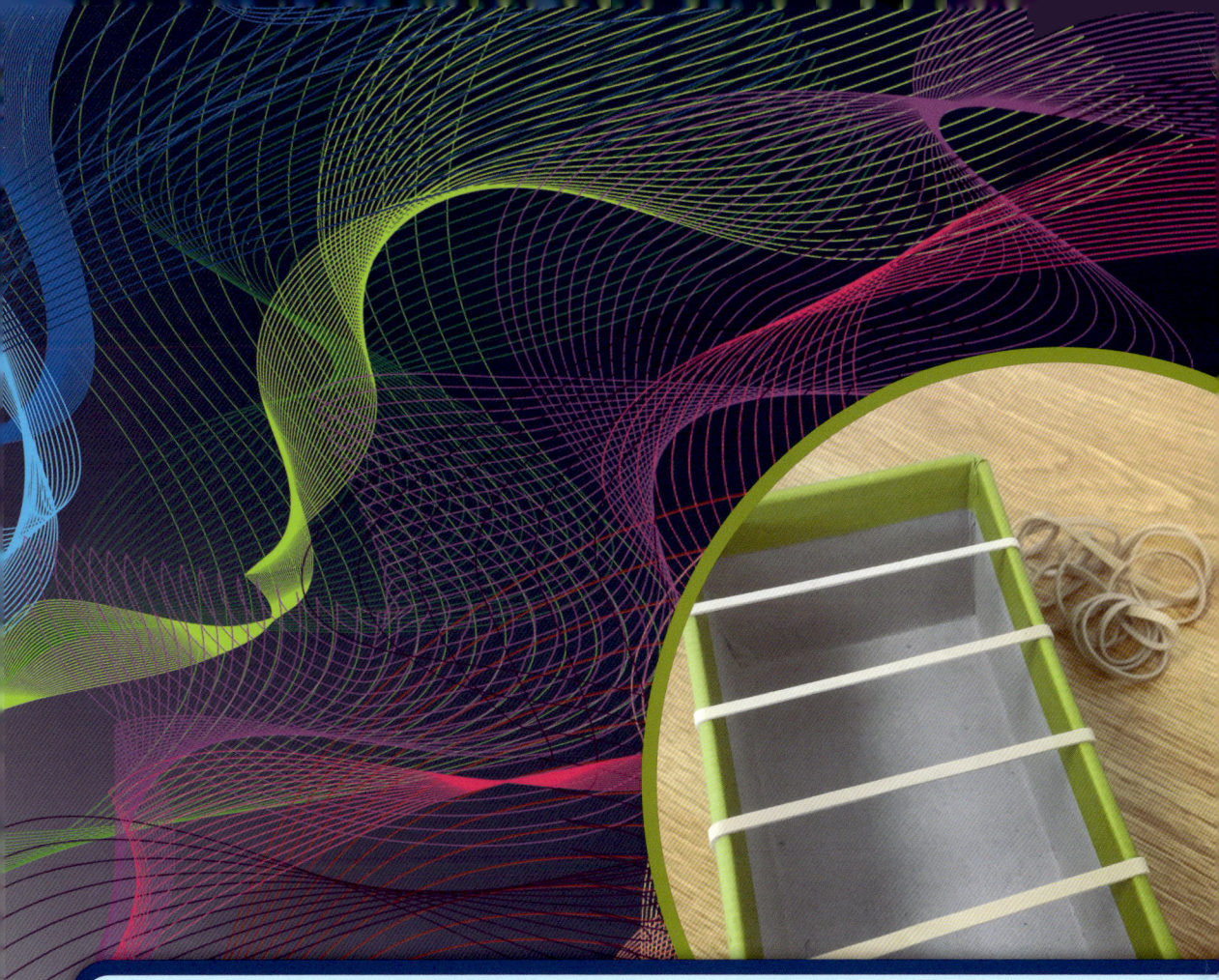

You can make your own musical instrument by stretching two rubber bands across a plastic box and plucking them with your fingers. The sounds will change if the rubber bands are made looser or tighter. It is like having your own guitar!

You can make music by whistling. Changing the position of your lips and tongue will change the sound of your whistle.

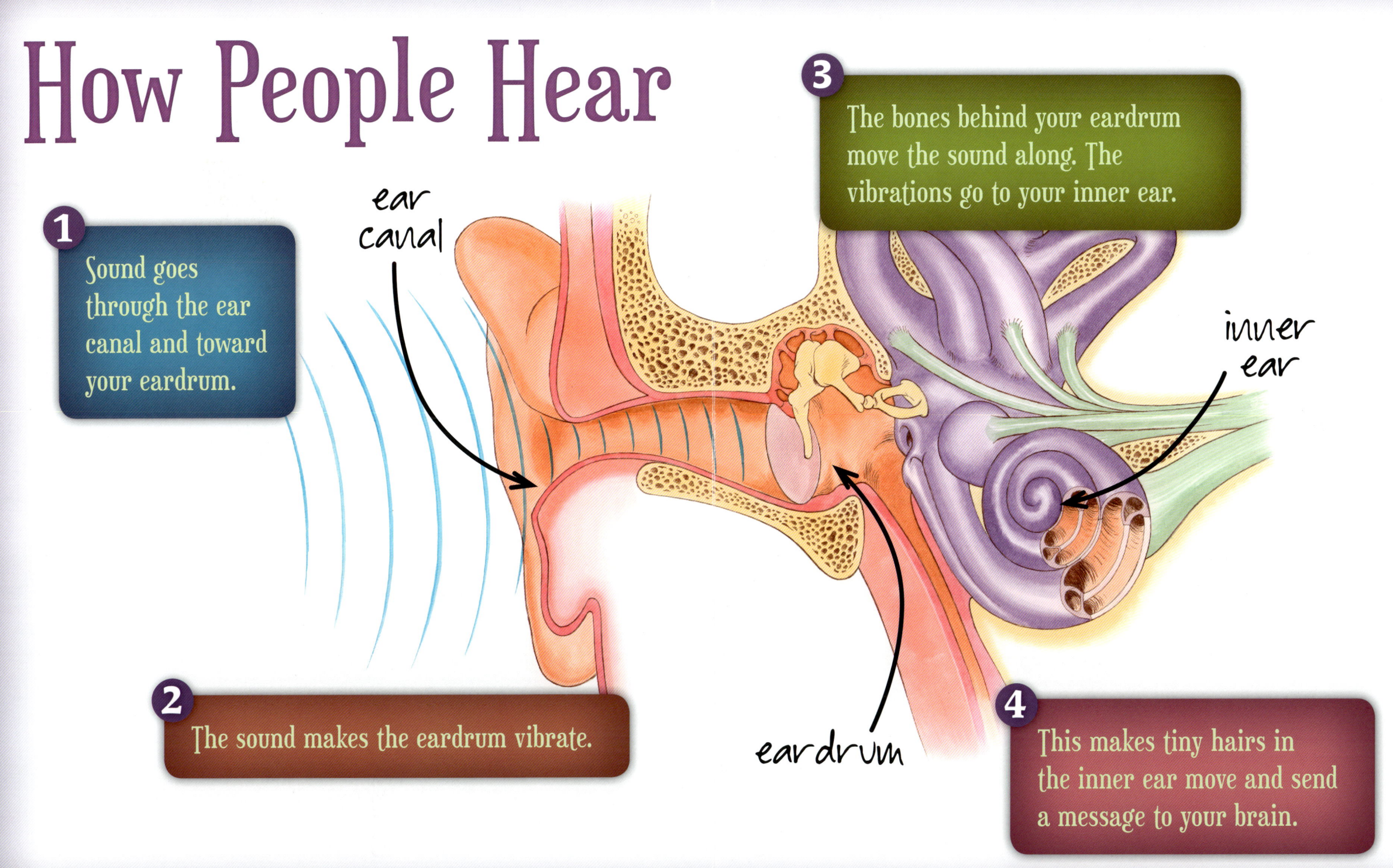

There is even a voice box inside your throat that can help you make music. Your voice box has two small muscles called **vocal cords**. They are like rubber bands. Vocal cords help you talk and sing.

When you breathe in, the air goes into your lungs. When you breathe out, the air blows across your vocal cords and causes them to vibrate, and the vibrations make sounds!

VOCAL CORDS

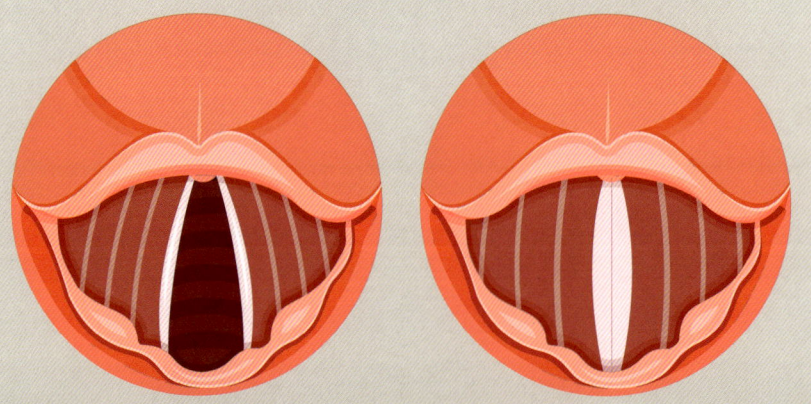

GLOSSARY

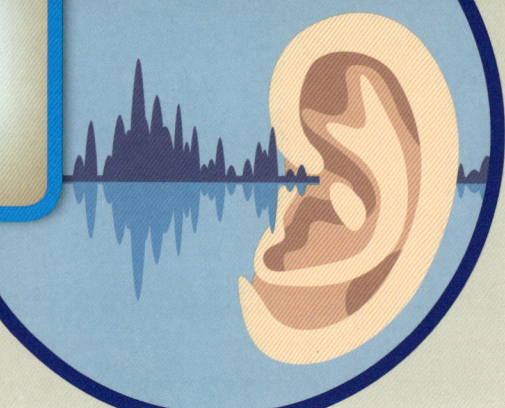

communicate
to give information to someone else, usually by speaking, writing, or moving your hands

echolocation
the use of sound waves and echoes to figure out where something is

particles
pieces of matter

vibration
a very quick back-and-forth motion

vocal cords
thin flaps inside the throat that allow people and animals to make sounds

INDEX

air 4–5, 7, 16, 19
bat 12–14
brain 6
communicate 3, 10
dolphin 15
echo 12
echolocation 12
flute 16
greater wax moth 13
guitar 16–17
hearing 8, 12–13
instruments 16–17
lightning 9
muscles 19
particles 4
rubber bands 17, 19
thunder 9
sound waves 5, 6
trumpet 16
vibration 4–6, 12, 14, 19
violin 16
vocal cords 19
waves 5
whales 14–15
whistling 18